Life's Journey

Life's Journey

BY:
Colonel Charles Dahnmon Whitt

Dahnmon Whitt Family Publishing

Post Office Box 831

Flatwoods, KY 41139

First Edition
Published: February 13, 2012

ISBN 978-1-62050-108-5

Phone 606-836-7997

E-Mail c-dahnmon@roadrunner.com

Web Site http://dahnmonwhittfamily.com/

1   *What am I doing here?*

Contents

Chapter	Page

Preface

This book is written to show you that you are not alone. It is also written to show you that you are loved.

Sure you have been in darkness but you can walk in the light and feel the peace of God.

I have revealed much about my life in this little book. I have been in darkness and I now walk in the light and have peace, joy, and confidence to live each day knowing who is watching over me and where I will live after this short stay here on God's Green Earth.

Read my little stories and see if any of them fit somewhere in your life. The secret of eternal life starting here on this earth is revealed in this book. The simple plan of salvation that Jesus gave us is unraveled in the simple writings of this book. I am not the answer but I hope to point you to the light.

What am I doing here?

The Beginning

Man has always questioned his purpose in life and where he is going! I hope to give you some insight as to our purpose, why we were created and where we are going.

Do we have destiny or do we just float around in the wind? I think both, but we have choices to make along the way.

I will be relying on personal experience and good old Bible teaching as to the answers I give.

The first book of the Bible, Genesis, tells us about the origins of everything, except God. God has always been and always will exist. God wanted people to commune with, to befriend, and walk and talk with. That is why he created the universe and made a man and woman.

Now are you going to believe the Word or God, which gives answers, or are you just going to meander on through life?

Let's see what God has to say about the beginning in His Book of Genesis.

This picture illustrates our struggle.

I'm betting on the Lord Jesus Christ.

What am I doing here?

Holy Reading, Genesis 1

1 In the beginning God created the heaven and the earth.

2 And the earth was without form and void; and darkness was upon the face of the deep. And the spirit of God moved upon the face of the waters.

3 And God said, let there be light and there was light.

4 And God saw the light, that it was good: and God divided the light from the darkness.

5 And God calls the light Day. And the darkness He called Night. And the evening and the morning were the first day.

6 And God said let there be a firmament in the mist of the waters, and let it divide the waters from the waters.

7 And God made the firmament, and divided the waters which were under the firmament

from the waters which were above the firmament: and it was so.

8 And God called the firmament Heaven. And the evening and the morning were the second day.

9 And God said, let the waters under the heaven be gathered together unto one place, and let the dry land appear: and it was so.

10 And God called the dry land Earth; and the gathering of the waters He called Sea; and God saw that it was good.

11 And God said, let the earth bring forth grass, the herb yielding seed, and the fruit tree yielding fruit after his kind, whose seed is in itself, upon the earth: and it was so.

12 And the earth brought forth grass, and herb yielding fruit, whose seed was in itself, after his kind: and God saw that it was good.

13 And the evening and the morning were the third day.

What am I doing here?

14 And God said, let there be lights in the firmament of the heaven to divide the day from the night; and let them be for signs, and for seasons, and for days, and years:

15 And let them be for lights in the firmament of the heaven to give light upon the earth; and it was so.

16 And God made two great lights: The greater light to rule the day and the lesser light to rule the night: he made the stars also.

17 And God set them in the firmament of the heaven to give light upon the earth.

18 And to rule over the day and over the night, and to divide the light from the darkness: and God saw that it was good.

19 And the evening and the morning were the fourth day.

20 And God said let the waters bring forth abundantly the moving creature that hath life and fowl that may fly above the earth in the open firmament of heaven.

21 And God created great whales, and every living creature that moveth, which the waters brought forth abundantly, after their kind, and every winged fowl after his kind: and God saw that it was good.

22 And blessed them, saying, be fruitful and multiply, and fill the waters in the seas and let fowl multiply in the earth.

23 And the evening and the morning were the fifth day.

24 And God said, let the earth bring forth the living creatures after his kind, cattle, and creeping thing, and beast of the earth after his kind: and it was so.

25 And God made the beast of the earth after his kind and cattle after their kind, and every thing that creepeth upon the earth after his kind: and God saw that it was good.

What am I doing here?

26 And God said; Let us make man in our image, after our likeness: and let them have dominion over the fish of the sea, and over the fowl of the air, and over the cattle, and over all the earth, and over every creeping thing that creepeth upon the earth.

27 So God created man in his own image, in the image of God created he him; male and female created he them. (To have a mind, and a free will)

Now here comes the problem. Sin entered mankind and we are all doomed to death, but we can rejoin God.

The Holy Bible Genesis 3

1 Now the serpent was more subtle than any beast of the field which God had made. And he said (devil) unto the woman, Yea, hath God said, Ye shall not eat of any tree of the garden?

2 And the woman said unto the serpent, Of the fruit of the trees of the garden we may eat:

3 but of the fruit of the tree which is in the midst of the garden, God hath said, Ye shall not eat of it, neither shall ye touch it, lest ye die.

4 And the serpent said unto the woman, Ye shall not surely die: (First Lie)

5 for God doth know that in the day ye eat thereof, then your eyes shall be opened, and ye shall be as God, knowing good and evil.

6 And when the woman saw that the tree was good for food, and that it was a delight to the eyes, and that the tree was to be desired to make one wise, she took of the fruit thereof, and did eat; and she gave also unto her husband with her, and he did eat.

7 And the eyes of them both were opened, and they knew that they were naked; and they sewed fig-leaves together, and made themselves aprons.

8 And they heard the voice of God walking in the garden in the cool of the day: and the man and his wife hid themselves from the

What am I doing here?

presence of God amongst the trees of the garden.

9 And God called unto the man, and said unto him, Where art thou?

10 And he said, I heard thy voice in the garden, and I was afraid, because I was naked; and I hid myself.

11 And he said, who told thee that thou wast naked? Hast thou eaten of the tree, whereof I commanded thee that thou shouldest not eat?

12 And the man said, The woman whom thou gavest to be with me, she gave me of the tree, and I did eat. (Man blamed the woman)

13 And God said unto the woman, What is this thou hast done? And the woman said, The serpent beguiled me, and I did eat.

14 And God said unto the serpent, because thou hast done this, cursed art thou above all cattle, and above every beast of the field;

upon thy belly shalt thou go, and dust shalt thou eat all the days of thy life:

15 and I will put enmity between thee and the woman, and between thy seed and her seed: he shall bruise thy head, and thou shalt bruise his heel.

16 Unto the woman he said, I will greatly multiply thy pain and thy conception; in pain thou shalt bring forth children; and thy desire shall be to thy husband, and he shall rule over thee.

17 And unto Adam he said, Because thou hast hearkened unto the voice of thy wife, and hast eaten of the tree, of which I commanded thee, saying, Thou shalt not eat of it: cursed is the ground for thy sake; in toil shalt thou eat of it all the days of thy life;

18 thorns also and thistles shall it bring forth to thee; and thou shalt eat the herb of the field;

19 in the sweat of thy face shalt thou eat bread, till thou return unto the ground; for

out of it wast thou taken: for dust thou art, and unto dust shalt thou return.

20 And the man called his wife's name Eve; because she was the mother of all living.

21 And God made for Adam and for his wife coats of skins, and clothed them.

22 And God said, Behold, the man is become as one of us, to know good and evil; and now, lest he put forth his hand, and take also of the tree of life, and eat, and live forever-

23 therefore God sent him forth from the Garden of Eden, to till the ground from whence he was taken.

24 So he drove out the man; and he placed at the east of the Garden of Eden the Cherubim, and the flame of a sword which turned every way, to keep the way of the tree of life.

Now does this sound like a fairy tale or something made up by someone that had too much wine?

Would you find it easier to believe if I used words like chromosomes, elements, atoms and electrons?

Right off the bat I would like to introduce you to the word "Faith". What is faith? It is "believing" and knowing something that is true even without concrete evidence. You know that chair you are sitting in will hold you up because you have tested it. By faith you sit down in it the first time, knowing it would hold you up.

John 3:
16 *For God so loved the world, that he gave his only begotten Son, that whosoever believeth on him should not perish, but have eternal life.*

17 *For God sent not the Son into the world to judge the world; but that the world should be saved through him.*

What am I doing here?

18 He that <u>believeth</u> on him is not judged: he that believeth not hath been judged already, because he hath not believed on the name of the only begotten Son of God.

God has given us answers about everything, yet we try to prove Him wrong with this theory and that theory.

Wouldn't it just be easier to believe God and enjoy the peace that comes with believing?

We are born into the world and have no choice as to who our mother and father are, yet we have a choice as to where we will spend eternity.

Born of Blood and Water

For you created my inmost being; you knit me together in my mother's womb.
Psalm 139:13

I was born, but I don't remember it. You were born and I bet you don't remember it either.

"Before I formed you in the womb I knew you, before you were born I set you apart;
Jeremiah 1:5

I was sent to my mother and father from God. They were to raise me upright and care for my physical needs as well.

If I remembered my birth, I may also remember from whence I came.

We all know how it works in this modern world, the love-making then the sperm enters the egg, and Wham, a baby is on the way. Where did the sperm and egg come from? God equipped us to reproduce and He puts the new earth bound baby into the sperm and the egg.

So if God creates each new little person, He also gives it the intellect to learn and to grow. He also adds one important thing. He adds to each new baby, the desire to search for and worship God.
People just can't help themselves; they want to worship something greater than themselves.

When people don't find God, there is emptiness in their lives; a void that needs to be filled.

This was hard on Adam and Eve, after they were sent away from the wonderful Garden of Eden. They could not walk with God and commune with Him as before. God was hurt; he had lost his friends through sin.

Of course Adam and Eve were hurt also. They were without their close friend, "God." They also had to earn their keep by working and fighting the evil things that now appeared upon the earth. Weeds, thistles, all kinds of insects, and even the animals turned against them.

In the garden they could eat fruit and walk among the great cats, bears, and other animals without fear. There was no hate or aggression in the animals before sin entered the world.

Some of the first things I can remember were pain and unhappiness. We are born crying! Then as I got older, I realized that there was love in the world.

My Mother and Father loved me, my brothers did also, except for a little jealousy. It seems that I was petted more and went to the doctor often. I was sickly and I now know why my mother and father were so protective of me. I had a beautiful big brother that had come to the world before me and in less than six months God called him back home with whooping cough.

Yes we are born of water and blood and we live our lives out that way. We are physical bodies that are constantly attacked by the things that sin brought upon us. The little invisible germs that sin brought fourth, and can attack us and cause destruction.

God's warning was not to disobey; Man and woman did disobey and were cast out of the garden and told that they shall surely die.

Folks, we have been dying ever since. When we are born, I believe we are on the road to physical death. We just don't want to die the spiritual death. That is the death that ends without Christ in our lives.

Could these Little Children Sin?
Do babies have sin?

Dahnmon and a Little Friend

Picture taken about 1949.

What am I doing here?

Do babies have sin?

Babies are not to the age of accountability, so they are counted without sin! Yet they have that natural born sin in their nature.

Sit two, two year olds, down and give them just one toy to share. You guessed it, they both want the toy and the stronger of the two will take it away.

Say a bad word in front of a baby that is just learning to talk and I bet he will learn the bad word.

Babies don't know any better than to do what is natural to them. They all have the instinct to whatever they want. They learn to look out for themselves at an early age. If they want something they go after it, they may scream and have a hissy-fit if they don't get it.

Does the baby sin, of course, but they are loved by God and He will not hold it against them until they reach that magic age; the age of accountability. What age is that? I think it varies as from person to person. Many folks say around twelve years of age. I think it may be earlier for some and later for others. It depends on how mature they are as to being open to the Holy Spirit.

Do you remember when you got your conscience? How old were you when you told that first lie, and knew it was wrong? How old were you when you hurt one of your friends to take something from them; and knew you had done wrong. That is when you knew you sinned.

I remember a time, way before I ever started to school, that I cried to get my way. I didn't know I was sinning, but after I got my hind-end spanked, I knew Mom and Dad were not happy with me.

Not much later I sinned in other ways; I and a little girl played together and found out that we had different parts. We were around 4 or 5 years old. I didn't think this was bad, until Dad asks me what I had been doing and I instantly lied, "Bam," I knew it was wrong to lie, so this was one of my first sins. I also learned not to be looking up little girl's dresses.

Of Course, the opposite sex has been the downfall of many men and women. Sexual desire enticed by the devil is a mighty strong force. That is why we are to have one wife and she is to love the husband. The wife is to have one husband and he is to love the wife. We in marriage are to forsake all others.

That is part of the problem today, men want more women and women want more men.

Train up a child in the way he should go: and when he is old, he will not depart from it.

Proverbs 22:6

My daddy was a devout Christian and he insisted that I go to Sunday school and Church. Not only I, but mommy, and my two brothers always went to the "Old White Church," in Raven, Virginia.

We didn't miss too many services as I remember. The old church was used by the Raven Methodist Church South for many years. It had a second story that the, "Red Men Lodge," used.

I have a lot of fond memories of the Old White Church. It had no indoor plumbing so you better wash and drink before you come to church. It did not have any central heating and air-conditioning either. The big "Pot-bellied," stove provided heat when needed. As you faced the old stove your front was too hot and your back was too cold. As for air-conditioning the big windows were raised if it got too hot. Some days it was still too hot.

What about other needs, it was outside around the corner and was called an outhouse or john.

<u>I do know and can affirm</u> that there was something else there at the Old White Church that we all needed. Jesus Christ went to church with us and the Holy Spirit spoke to all of us.

I must admit, at first, I just went because dad and mom took me. I developed many good memories at that old white church.

Even at an early age I rebelled against God.

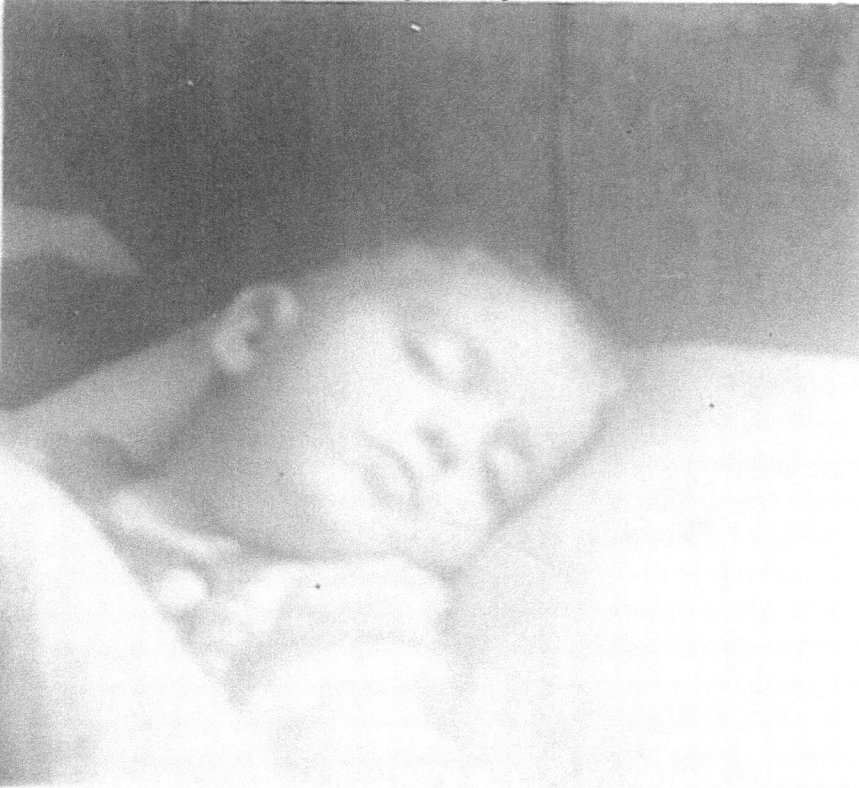

Young Dahnmon around 1945 in Raven,
Virginia

**Dahnmon at about 1948
Before the age of Accountability**

This is the Old White Church!
Raven Methodist Church South!
Raven, Virginia
What am I doing here?

Did I always do what was pleasing to mommy and daddy? Nope, I had to learn the hard way about a lot of things.

I was a sickly child with a lot to encounter during my first years. I was born breach and have been backward ever since.

 I had the jaundice when I was born and mom was not too proud of me. Later I had rheumatic fever and worried mom and dad. Later I remember at about the age of seven I had spinal meningitis. Mommy and daddy had lost the baby before me. Joseph Edward Whitt was a healthy little boy that came down with whooping caught and died. I hope to meet him in Heaven someday. By losing Joe Ed, they were really cautious about my watch care. I guess I gave them many things to be concerned about.

The Polio epidemic was running rampant at this time and I had to stay in and rest a lot. Mom thought if I stayed rested I wouldn't get it. Soon the vaccine came out and the concern soon ended.

Life's Journey

This picture is Dahnmon at the grave of little Joseph Edward Whitt.

For my spinal meningitis, I first blamed my dad. Poor dads, they get the blame for many things, don't they? A friend and I were playing under an apple tree in late summer with a lot of early apples on the ground. We would swing on a low limb and land on the ground. You guessed it, the apples had attracted a lot of bees and I found one. I landed on that little bee and it had its stinger aimed right at my foot. I yelled out loudly and mom came running. When she found out it was only a bee sting and I yelled like I cut my foot off, she gave me a good spanking for scaring her so badly. Now

What am I doing here?

I was stung, my hind-end was burning, now dad made me help the family pick strawberries. (I probably ate more than I put in the pail.)

Next morning I was running a high fever and my neck hurt really badly. I thought it was picking those old strawberries that dad made me do that had caused my pain and suffering.

Daddy and mommy rushed me to the hospital and I was down for several days. I was out of my head, but I do remember my brothers, Jerry and Larry looking in the door at me. They were not allowed to come in because I was highly contagious.

Now I remember something of importance, the word got out to all the little churches that a young boy laid close to death; and many saints prayed for me. I saw God in action at that early age. God answered prayer and I am here writing this book to prove it.

I surprised everyone when I was around seven years of age. Daddy and mommy had been going to the Pentecostal Church, but were not happy with their feelings and decided to go to Raven Methodist. After some time they decided to join there and serve to their best abilities. They were called up front to take their vows to serve God and the Church. As they stood there, guess who was standing beside them? Yep, it was me. They did not know I was going to stand with them. Was I too young? I guess not, I joined the church that day and learned more about serving God. I think I had reached the age of accountability at age seven. Was I a mature Christian? Nope, I was a beginner that believed in God. I can't remember when I didn't believe there was a God.

My brothers also believed in God. I had heard them both say something about God often.

Jerry was called on to pray in church one time as a teen and he was a bit befuzzled, but he got through it.

I was about 8 or 9 I think when Larry my other big brother first called on me to help with his paper route. He would only call on me if he was running late or in a hurry for some reason.

Larry, about 13, had a big paper route that covered several miles, and he did it all on his trusty bike.

He was up early each morning and headed up the dirt road we lived on in Stinson Bottom. It was up hill about a quarter of a mile to the Old White Church, where they dropped off his papers each morning. After spending time rolling up the papers and placing them in the two bags, he would coast down the hill into West Raven and deliver all of them. Next he would climb the hill by the Church again and coast down the east side into the little town of Raven. He worked his way through backside of the little town and into Red Ash a little coal camp. He delivered to all of the customers in Red Ash Hollow and up another big hill to the main road, Route U.S. 460. He delivered to that area and coasted down the big hill probably gaining a speed of forty miles an hour back into the front part of Raven. Next he would cover the lower end of Doran. Then he would transverse Raven Hill back to the old Raven Methodist Church where he had started. It was downhill from there and he had customers down the hill and more around the circle of homes on the two dirt roads off the main dirt road. (About two blocks) and he was home and had to get ready for school.

I remember the first time he called on me to help. He got me awake and helped me to get dressed. I was not too enthused about the idea. It would be dark out there and I was afraid of the dark. I was always afraid of the dark and many other things. Mom said it was due to my bout with rheumatic fever. All I know is that I was afraid.

We were raised in a Christian home and I knew about God and all of his power, but I also knew it was scary out on these country roads with not a sign of a street light. I had even heard of ghosts playing around the old White Church during the dark hours.

I stuck close to Larry and helped him roll his papers, and my job was to go back down into Stinson Bottom and take care of our neighbor customers. I didn't want to leave the security of my big brother, and head out into the darkness even though I had a flashlight.

Larry told me something that morning that has stuck with me for over fifty years.

"Dahnmon, God will protect you when you pray and ask him to. It will even help to sing out loud, God Will Protect Me," Larry explained.

Finally Larry headed down into West Raven and I headed down into Stinson Bottom singing about as loud as I could, "God will protect me!"

I felt the calmness of God that morning in my young life; I still pray for His protection.

It must have been some sight, the little boy flashing his light back and forth and singing as loud as possible, "God will protect me!"

I owe a lot to my Brothers, Mom, Dad, and Almighty God!

Did I always stay close to God? Nope, I am a creation of God with a free spirit and I drifted away from God many times as I wanted to taste the so called joys of the world. Many of these tastes are not good for us as Eve found out in the garden.

What am I doing here?

My Family About 1949 at Camden Park

What am I doing here?

Crying To Go Fishing

We all want our way! Old and young alike want to have their way!

I remember it like it was yesterday, that first wiggly Rainbow Trout I had in my slick hands.

It all started the year before when I was a first grader. Trout season opened in western Virginia at noon in early April. Back then people in the area would take off work to enjoy the stocked mountain streams in the western counties. My daddy did not miss work very much but he must have really enjoyed the annual opening day of trout season. I remember as he prepared to go fishing that day, I wanted to go with him so bad. (I cried to go)

He knew the mountain terrain and rugged trout streams were not the place for a first grader on opening day. Even though I put up a demanding performance of tears and pleading I was left behind. Daddy did halfway promise that I could go the next year.

What am I doing here?

Daddy left with his store bought cane pole and seemed to be gone forever. I waited with great anticipation for his return, because I knew he would have some of the beautiful Rainbow Trout for me to look at and even eat, even though I did not like fish very much.

Sure enough when daddy got home he had three of the most beautiful fish I had ever saw. I remember them as really big, but like everything else, things are big to a first grader. I was so proud of my Dad's accomplishment, and just knew I could catch some if I just had a chance.

Back to my fish story, daddy did let me go when I was in the second grade. It was a beautiful spring day as I remember it. I was all excited and had my little green pole that daddy cut from the brush along the way. He attached the black fishing line about half way down the pole. Then he tied it again at the very top of the green sapling. He explained that if a fish broke my pole he would still be tied at the center. Daddy was very smart like that.

Daddy packed us some sandwiches and stuff in a brown bag, got our night crawlers, and we headed for Wolf Creek. This is some of the most rugged country in Virginia.

Daddy told me to be really careful because of the rough conditions, but I thought I was a tough boy in the second grade. When we got to Wolf Creek Dad let me fish by myself, but he stayed close so he could do a rescue if he needed to.

The little leafs were just starting to grow and the mountain Dogwoods were blooming. There was much greenery even this early in the spring due to the Mountain Laurel, and Hemlocks. The rocks were so slick, as if God had given them a greasing. As soon as we left the car I started a trend for the day, fall down and get up. Dad thought it was funny, but still was afraid I would get hurt.

"Now Son, be careful, if you get hurt we will have to go home," Daddy said.

I had what they call fisherman's luck, "A wet tail and a hungry gut."

Now back then the season did not open until twelve noon, so we all got our tackle ready and had a bite to eat. Then we put on a night crawler and waited for the magical hour to drop our baits to the awaiting trout. The game wardens were walking up and down the banks disguised as fishermen trying to catch somebody dropping a hook in too early. They wore fishing clothes and had flies on their hats. Daddy pointed them out to me and warned me not to start too early. He said to watch him, and when he started fishing for me to start also. I could hardly wait.

Finally we were fishing in earnest along with about every other men and boys in the western end of Virginia. People were getting their lines tangled with each other, and some were slipping and sliding almost as much as me.

People started yanking out the flopping fish

and I even got a bite or two. I was too slow to hook the sneaky things. Daddy had three or four nice trout and I still had not caught my first.

I did the forbidden thing in fishing, I moved in on two fellers that were having really good luck. (Fishing Sin)They gave me a dirty look but didn't say anything. I baited up and flipped my worm out among the hungry trout and sure enough one wanted it. I yanked on the little green pole and the trout landed right in my hands against my chest. The wrestling match was on as I tried to hold on to the slippery Rainbow Trout. I bet that was a real show to the other fishermen. As I remember it, it was a big one, but I lost the battle, it was free once again in Wolf Creek.

I was exasperated at giving my prized catch its freedom, and just stood there for a long moment. I probably sinned again with the thought of, "S__T." I remember I started to trudge to the bank to get another worm, but one of the fishermen gave me another worm so I would just be still. (I was making too much disturbance) (Another fishing sin) I didn't get another fish that year, but I felt some comfort in knowing I had a whopper in my hands. Remember what I said about things looking big when you are a kid!

The day went fast and it was time to go home. Daddy had six nice sized Rainbows and we headed to the car. I was totally worn out after fighting the rough ground, slick rocks and a whopper trout. (Lied about how big it was)(Fishing sin)

Daddy consoled me and said there would be other trips. He explained that I needed a landing net, even though he had none of his own. Sure enough the next year came and I was there with my new landing net. Guess what, I caught not one trout, but two. Daddy and I never missed an opening day of trout season until I left for the Navy.

Raising Rabbits

I was around ten years old when daddy let me purchase a pet rabbit from the Joyce boys. They were our neighbors not too far away. The Joyce boys were my friends and enemies, according to what day it was. But that is another story. Now back to the Bunny Tale.

I got some chicken wire and built a pen, and also a cage up off the ground with hardware cloth in the bottom. This was in there so when my rabbit did his business the little pellets fell out on the ground. I learned that from the Joyce boys.

As time went by, my Pete grew up and he was a girl rabbit, to my surprise. The Joyce boys told me I should bring her out for a visit and let her get bred, that way I could have little baby bunnies for sale. The idea sounded pretty good to me, so I took her courting out at the Joyce boys' house. I did not bother to ask Daddy, I just knew he would like the idea. If I sold the new babies

I could give him some money for feed and pen making stuff.

I found out, rabbits get their babies real quick, about three weeks. Somehow I got it in my head that mommy rabbits always have babies in increments of seven. I don't remember how I learned this important thing, dreamed it or maybe the Joyce boys.

I told daddy that I took Pete courting, (Things I had learned, and I knew better) and daddy was not as pleased about it as I was. I told him that Pete would have seven babies before long.

"Now you don't know she will have seven babies!" Daddy said.

"When did you take her out there?" he asked.

"About two weeks ago I reckon, and yes she will get seven babies," I said insistently.

Daddy just shook his head and smiled as if

to say, "Wait and see."

Now you have to picture this, daddy bought all the fencing, boards, and nails, not to mention food for my rabbit. Now she was going to be a mommy rabbit.

The short gestation period for rabbits is only three weeks and it passed quickly. I went out one morning and Pete had dug a hole under a board in the floor of the pen. She had pulled all the fur off her chest and had lost substantial weight. I investigated the situation and was pleased to be the owner of seven new bunny babies. I couldn't wait for daddy to get home from work to tell him the good news. I also wanted him to know that mommy rabbits do always have seven babies the first time.

When daddy got home that evening in his normal coal dirty clothes and black face, I ran to greet him and tell about Pete having babies. (Daddy was a coal miner)

"Daddy, Pete had seven babies just like I told

you," I said proudly.

"She did, now that is just a coincidence that she had seven," Daddy replied.

After daddy had his bath and eat supper, mommy and he went out to see Pete's babies.

"They sure are cute little things," mommy said.

I agreed and reemphasized that she had seven just like I said.

Even Mommy agreed with Daddy, rabbits don't always have seven babies the first time. Didn't Pete just prove that they do, I thought.

Time went on and the babies grew up quickly. The Joyce boys suggested I bring Pete courting again. (I knew better, Dad had already shown displeasure of my new bunny family.)It sounded like a splendid idea; I could picture the fourteen new bunny babies in my young mind.

Daddy had not complained about buying
rabbit food for the now eight rabbits I had.
After I took Pete courting again I told daddy
about the new development and that Pete
was expecting fourteen new baby bunnies.
(Daddy was not happy with my sneaking
around.) Daddy did not share the
excitement and anticipation that I did.

Now daddy disagreed with me again about
how many babies mommy rabbits have.

Sometimes mommies and daddies seem so
dumb, I thought.

Daddy implied he would not be too happy
with all the new little mouths to feed.
Fourteen I knew. (Plus the 8 I already had)

In no time at all Pete got fat and pulled the
fur off her chest again. I went out one
morning to find Pete had babies again. I
pulled out all the new little arrivals and
counted each one. Guess what, she had

fourteen new bunny babies. As before I could hardly wait to tell Daddy when he got home from the mine. As soon as he got home I ran to tell him of the grand news. (Mother rabbit's line their nest with the fur from their chest.)

"Pete had babies last night," I told with much pride.

"How many did she have?" Daddy asked as if to prove a point.

"Fourteen," I said proudly.

"Don't you know that mommy rabbits always have fourteen babies the second time?" I asked as a pro rabbit breeder.

"That is just a coincidence," Daddy insisted.

Now Pete had proved that mommy rabbits always have fourteen the second time, not to mention that she proved they have seven the first time. After a couple of weeks passed I mentioned that Pete would have twenty one babies next time.

"Oh no, she wouldn't, you are not taking Pete courting anymore," Dad said in no uncertain terms.

I now had twenty two rabbits, guess what; Daddy wanted me to get rid of some of my baby bunnies.

I guess me and Pete finally convinced daddy that mommy rabbits have babies in increments of seven!

I felt sad that I had been dishonest with daddy as I had gone behind his back to take "Pete" courting again.

What am I doing here?

More Sins

For my twelfth birthday, mommy gave me a Daisy Defender BB Gun, with certain stipulations. I had to agree not to shoot at any birds. I agreed spontaneously so I could get my hands on the new air rifle. The Daisy Defender was a special model BB gun; it had a magazine like the pump models and only held fifty BB's. It was also more powerful than most air rifles.

"Now son, if I ever hear of you shooting birds I will take your BB gun, and you will never get it back," Mommy told me.

"I promise, I won't shoot birds," I answered quickly. (A promise I meant to keep, but I yielded to temptation.)

"Here is your birthday present, please be careful with it," Mommy said as she handed me the most precious gift a boy could get.

I took the new air rifle everywhere I went during the next few days, and did not even think of shooting at any live targets. As time went on I became quiet proficient with the great little rifle. All the boys were envious of my treasure. I could shoot farther and more accurate than any of my friends.

After several months passed the temptation grew, and I yielded. My neighbors the Kennedy's, saved scraps of food for their hogs. They had a bucket hanging at the end of their clothes line. We called it a slop bucket back then. The bucket was up out of reach of dogs, cats, and other critters that may want to feed upon the enticing morsels. The bucket did attract a long line of black birds that lined up on the clothes line. This was my temptation, and one day I could not resist. (I went back on my word and sinned again.)

I had to be stealth, not to get a shot at the birds, but not to get caught. This day only one black bird set on the line close to the slop bucket. I looked at my house, my grandmother's house and roundabout for any witness that may report an unauthorized shooting. The coast was clear so I took the opportunity to try my air rifle on a living, breathing bird. (Trying to hide my sins)

I gave one more, quick look around, raised the rifle and aimed at the feathered target. I squeezed the trigger and the deadly missile was on the way. What happened next was unbelievable; I hit the black bird in the head and killed it instantly. It didn't fall to the ground; it had a death grip on the clothes line and just hung there upside down, as evidence of my mischief. The bird kept swinging back and forward to torment me.

I panicked, I had to get that bird to turn loose of the clothes line and hide the evidence. I laid down my prized weapon and ran in a bolt toward the swinging bird. I jumped up and hit the bird with my hand to knock it down, and this only caused it to swing round and round.

Oh my, this bird was determined to wreak revenge on its slayer. What was I going to do? I jumped with all my might with both hands extended and caught the bird with a death grip. With all my weight and might I yanked the bird free of the clothes line. I threw the dead thing over in the weeds to hide the evidence. I looked all around and as far as I could tell, no one saw this crime but Almighty God. (I had gone back on my word and killed one of God's little birds.)

I was instantly sorry for my actions, it was the first thing I had ever killed, and I was sorry about that. I was also sorry for breaking my promise to Mommy. My crime was hidden; I would just have to live with it.

Almost fifty years later when Mommy was in poor health and not too long for this world, I confessed the whole thing to her. She smiled and said you have been punished enough by keeping this secret for all of these years. I knew I was forgiven, and felt relieved for killing the swinging black bird. I can still see that bird hanging upside down and swinging back and forth, in my mind.

What am I doing here?

Does God Give Us A Way Out?

Romans 3:

22 *even the righteousness of God through* <u>*faith in Jesus Christ*</u> *unto all them that believe; for there is no distinction;*

23 *for* <u>*all have sinned*</u>*, and fall short of the glory of God;*

24 *being* <u>*justified freely by his grace*</u> *through the redemption that is in Christ Jesus:*

I am truly thankful that Jesus died for me and I can be washed whiter than snow. I am not a murderer, but to God all sin is sin.

If we are honest, we must admit that we have lied, cheated, stole, and gossiped. Even that little white lie is sin. According to that verse Romans 3:23 we all have sinned and are in need of forgiveness.

So was it a sin to sneak around, and disobey mommy, and take the life of that blackbird? Sure it was, even if I was just ten years old. I knew better and my conscience told me I was wrong. I even tried to cover up the evidence by getting that bird off the clothes line. I kept it hid for over fifty years, but I needed to confess it to mommy.

Thank God, He does not hold us accountable for our sin after we accept Christ as our Savior. He doesn't even remember our sin.

When someone hurts us, we can forgive them, but I doubt you will forget it.

What Price?

What "Price" will you give? Don't worry it's free!

Is there really a Heaven? Is there really a Hell?

God wrote the word, it is for us to read!

If God wrote the word, it is for us to read!

If God wrote the word, it is for us to heed!

Yes there is a Heaven, the price has been paid!

Yes there is a Hell! For those that don't heed, their fate is made!

So remember with Jesus the price has been paid!

So remember with Satan our fate is made!

Relying On God

While camping with my Scout Troop at the park on High Knob Mountain near Coeburn Virginia, It rained like a Monsoon. After a day and two nights of staying in leaky Pup Tents, our Scout Master W.W. Smith had enough! He went to a phone to call a friend that had a Hunters Cabin on out the Mountain in some of the most Primitive land east of the Mississippi River. The man told W. W. Smith that he was welcome to take the troop to the cabin, and relayed the location of the hidden key.

We broke camp that wet morning, loaded up our wet stuff and headed out for another new adventure. Back in these days deer and other game was scarce, but not on High Knob. Most of us had never seen a deer out in the wild before. As we traveled out the little mountain road we counted over twenty deer as we passed.

Guess what, the rain stopped as we came up on the little cabin. As we got out of the little bus, the first thing we saw in the soft ground was, Bear Tracks! Wow, this sent fear abounding into every boy there, and probably our Scout Master too! Of course he tried to calm our souls by telling us that a bear would not bother a bunch of noisy boys. This did not help us too much!

We moved into the cabin with all our gear. There was about a dozen of us. We only had enough floor space for all the boys to lie down.

There was no water or plumbing, so Rev. W.W.Smith (Scoutmaster) told me and Frankie to stay at the cabin and watch our stuff, while he took all the other boys on an expedition to look for drinking water.

After all the boys left Frankie and I were quiet scared there by ourselves. We were both church goers and I had a little Bible in my gear. I don't remember how I knew about the 91st Psalms, but I turned there and begin to read God's word!

The 91st Psalm is all about how God gives his followers protection. This was soothing to our souls, in a time of distress. After reading the word Frankie and I had a little prayer meeting up on the mountain sitting there in that little cabin. We were still alert, but were not so scared after our talk with God.

It wasn't long before we heard a commotion as all the boys came running back to the cabin. They had had a frightful encounter with a large Black Bear out in the woods.

They gave us a report that they came up on him and he lowered his head and extended his neck while letting out a loud growl. The bruin never offered to back up or run. This was his mountain and he would defend it if it came to that. The boys panicked and ran in different directions all leading to the shelter of the Hunter's Cabin! W.W. Smith tried not to show alarm, but was on the heels of the running scouts.

We all decided we did not want to build a

fire outside of the cabin to cook our suppers. So we all sit in the cabin eating various canned foods cold and right out of the cans. I never will forget I opened a can of spaghetti, dumped it into my surplus mess kit which had some spilled soap powders in it. I never noticed the soap until I begin to eat. I ate around the soap the best I could.

Our Scout Master tried to act brave and even said he was going to put his sardine can outside the door to attract the bear. He was always fooling with us like that. I did notice he stayed in the cabin with the rest of us.

We had a restless night and when we got up to go outside for latrine purposes, the first thing we saw was fresh bear tracks that led to the cabin! That insolent bruin had followed the running scouts right to the cabin! Needless to say we were alert that morning.

Our Scout Master decided to move us one more time. He knew about a church camp over in Lee County, Virginia that was open and not too far away. We never let on about being scared, but none complained about packing up and heading off the mountain and wilds of High Knob.

This was just another time in my young life that I called upon the God of Creation in a time of trouble and fear.

Psalms 91

1 He that dwelleth in the secret place of the Most High Shall abide under the shadow of the Almighty.

2 I will say of Jehovah, He is my refuge and my fortress; My God, in whom I trust.

3 For he will deliver thee from the snare of the fowler, And from the deadly pestilence.

4 He will cover thee with his pinions, (feathers) And under his wings shalt thou take refuge: His truth is a shield and a buckler.

5 Thou shalt not be afraid for the terror by night, Nor for the arrow that flieth by day;

6 For the pestilence that walketh in darkness, Nor for the destruction that wasteth at noonday.

7 A thousand shall fall at thy side, And ten thousand at thy right hand; But it shall not come nigh thee.

8 Only with thine eyes shalt thou behold, And see the reward of the wicked.

9 For thou, O Jehovah, art my refuge! Thou hast made the Most High thy habitation;

10 There shall no evil befall thee, Neither shall any plague come nigh thy tent.

<u>11 For he will give his angels charge over thee, To keep thee in all thy ways.</u>

12 They shall bear thee up in their hands, Lest thou dash thy foot against a stone

What am I doing here?

13 Thou shalt tread upon the lion and adder: The young lion and the serpent shalt thou trample under foot.

14 Because he hath set his love upon me, therefore will I deliver him: I will set him on high, because he hath known my name.

15 He shall call upon me, and I will answer him; I will be with him in trouble: I will deliver him, and honor him.

16 With long life will I satisfy him, and show him my salvation.

This scripture has been dear to me for many years as it has given me strength in times of danger.

God has always been there, when I wasn't too stubborn or stupid to ask His help.

Another Time I Called On God

My first real deer hunt brought out some doubts, fears, and bravery. It all took place in the Carroll County Virginia Mountains. I was with an older friend by the name of Reece. I was about sixteen and Reece was in his upper forties. I had met him while I worked at the Raven Super Market.

Reece was a typical redneck, and had built a forerunner to the modern truck camper. It was a plywood contraption built on his old pickup. He had two beds and a little laundry stove for heat. I thought it was all built masterfully. The day came, a Sunday morning, and we headed out across Route 16, and across the three high mountains to Marion, Virginia. To a flatlander, this is scarier than a ride on the biggest roller coaster ever made. Reece drove carefully up each mountain, using a lot of gas, (27 cents per gallon) then he would shut off the engine and coast all the way to the bottom. I was just too youthful to be afraid of such tactics.

What am I doing here?

We left on Sunday, which gave us time to set up camp and scout out a place to hunt on Monday morning when the deer season actually opened. Virginia was really strict about its game laws and also speed limits in the early sixties. We kept our rifles and shot guns in their cases on Sunday; they had already been checked out, fired and cleaned the week before.

We got over to the Carroll County Mountains and set up Reece's prized camper by pulling one side up on a rock to level her out. Then after eating some bologna sandwiches we went out into the woods and staked out a spot for in the morning. During the day we ran into some other hunters from our little village of Raven, VA One of them had just bought an International Scout, a nifty little four wheel drive. They didn't have four wheelers back in the early sixties. I ran into Jack the owner of the Scout a day later, he was straddle a log down in the woods, and could not get the front wheels locked in. I helped him rock it a bit and he finally got the front locked in and climbed across the log.

The night before we went into the woods for the first hunt we checked out our licenses, and I noticed that I had a bear tag as well as a deer tag. Reece told me that there were bears in these mountains, and if I saw one it was fair game. This made me think about the possibility of bringing home a bear. I knew that bears are dangerous critters, and you better have a good shot if you wanted to bag one. The old saying rings true, "Sometimes you get the bear, and sometimes the bear gets you!"

Now for my rifle, it was big as a small cannon. I had purchased it from Sears by mail order for $10.88. It was a surplus British 303. This was before the laws had changed, due to the assassination of President Kennedy. The only stipulation was that Sears did not sell to minors. Dad had given me permission to order the big rifle. A year or two earlier I wanted to get one, but I read that they did not sell to minors. I asked Daddy why he couldn't order a rifle. Daddy was a coal miner, why would they discriminate against miners I questioned? Dad had a good laugh on that one. I had the two words confused. Miners and Minors of course mean entirely two different things.

Well anyway, I had this big gun that held ten bullets in the clip and one in the chamber. The bullets were rated bigger that the American 30-06 and had 215 grain bullets. Shucks, if I could hit it, it would bring down an elephant. So I felt confident about having fire power even for a big bear.

The next morning we were up hours before sunrise, ate a hurried breakfast as we warmed by the little laundry stove. We put on several layers of warm clothing to ward off the below freezing mountain air. Next we took our flashlights and headed out toward our deer stands. It was exciting as we noticed flashlights all around the mountains, the hunters lights reminded us of fireflies as they headed to a place to hunt. The trails did not look anything like they did in the light of the day before. About first light the high powered rifles and shot guns began to rang out. I heard one that reminded me of someone tearing overall britches. If you heard one shot, usually it would be followed by one or two more as the deer ran past numerous hunters. I still had limited visibility; it is always darker in the mountain woods. I could hear deer running but never saw a one that morning. The season was for bucks only, but I think that many of the crazy hunters were shooting at anything that moved. Some of the hunters were hung over from a night of drinking and poker playing. As I sat there watching the fog freeze on my rifle barrel, I realized why deer hunting was so dangerous. I did see a scared doe up in the day as she was hauling the mail right toward me; I began to wonder if she was going to run right over me. She saw me as I began to move out of the way, and she did a 180 degree turn in midair.

Next day went about the same, except I saw many squirrels playing in the trees. After lunch on the second day I pulled out my

1948 Topper H & R twenty gauge shotgun
and killed a squirrel for supper. After
supper we sat around talking and planning
the hunt for the third and last day of our
hunt. Reece thought we might be better off
hunting over on the other ridge, which we
had not even been on. We had no time to
explore; we would be traveling in unknown
woods with only our little flashlights to
illuminate the sparse trails. The mountains
had an abundance of Laurel and thickets.
We trudged along until the trail split, Reece
took the one to the right and I took the left
which leveled off slightly. It was pitch dark
at this parting, but I could see the sky
lightening up way off in the East by the
coming dawn. It was like being in another
world.   I traveled about one third of a mile
up the slightly rising trail. Each minute that
passed brought a little more light to the
mountain.

I started looking for a place to have my
stand, and found a rotting log that had been
torn apart by some strong force. As I shined
my light to investigate, a great big bear track

stood out, in the loose dirt. I looked closer
to realize that a bear had torn open the
rotting log to feed upon the bugs and worms
it held. My heart jumped and fluttered a
little bit to the realization that I was in the
dark woods with a big bear. I whispered a
prayer to God as quickly as I could. I asked
God to be with me and protect me from
harm. I felt His presence in the dark woods
and felt better.

It was still too dark to really get a good aim
with the old 303. I began to scan the area
around me. I turned 360 degrees slowly
looking hard into the dim woods. I looked
again at the dismantled log and bear tracks.
I looked around and to the right slightly
behind me, and about fifty yards up the
ridge I saw something that made my heart
jump again. My Lord, there is that big black
bear I thought. It was just standing there
looking toward the new morning light.

What to do? What to do? Should I wait for
more light? Should I sneak back down the
trail, or should I start a stalking hunt and

shoot this trophy with my big rifle? It was still a little too dark to aim through the conventional sights on the old British 303. Was I scared?

Yes I was scared, but I began to compose myself, with God's help, and was quite pleased with the prospect of going home to Raven, Virginia, with a big bear. I thought about my fire power, and the ever increasing light. "Be brave," I told myself, God is with me.

I began to stalk the big black thing, I moved like a Cherokee Brave through the dim woodland. I carefully placed each foot, not to break a twig or rattle the leaves on the woodland floor. It was still too dark for a long shot, I knew I had to get really close, or have much more light to let off a round from the big 303. My adrenaline was rushed about as far as it could go. I gripped the big rifle and quietly took of the safety. I had covered more ground than I realized, then I looked about again. It was getting much lighter now which relieved me to know I could aim much better now. I was only about fifteen yards from the black form waiting for me. With the added light of the new dawn and my closeness, I strained my every fiber to see the big bear.

Oh my, it was not a bear at all; it was an ancient black stump. Had God moved the bear or was I just nuts? I felt really weird, bewildered, and relieved at the same time. I felt foolish, yet really proud to know that I could face the giant bear, with God's help, even though it was just a stump. It looked like a bear in the dim light of the Carroll County woods. Sure enough, there had been a bear about!

Let a man meet a bear robbed of her cubs,
Rather than a fool in his folly.
PROVERBS 17:12

Even as dangerous as a mommy bear is, our folly is more dangerous!

What am I doing here?

Brave Or Just Trusting God?

While serving in the United States Navy, at Oceana Naval Air Station in the summer of 1966 I went through an ordeal. This was a Master Jet Base in Virginia Beach Virginia serving the fleet during the Viet Nam War. The squadrons of fighters and attack aircraft were based here while the Aircraft Carriers were in home port at Norfolk Naval Base.

I was part of what we called Ship's Company, and we had about twelve aircraft assigned to us to maintain and we also took care of transient aircraft coming in with problems. We called these problems "Gripes"!

The summer of 1966, I was an Aviation Structural Mechanic 3rd class. I was of the sheet metal type which dealt mostly with an aircraft's body (fuselage), air controls, and the like. There were two other types of Aviation Structural mechanic's, these were hydraulics, and safety equipment such as ejection seats. We all intermingled as needed. All three types had a basic idea about the others. I happened to be on duty this summer day, when a Navy F-9 from another base, landed with a hydraulic gripe.

The pilot announced he was losing hydraulic fluid somehow, and he wanted it fixed ASAP, so he could get airborne again. Chief Hewlett the line chief had a quick fix which alarmed the pilot and me as I would be involved.

Normally we would pull an aircraft into the hanger, set it up on jacks, and hook up a Hydraulic Jenny. (Pump) This way the controls could be worked and any leaks would become obvious. This was the correct way to deal with such problems.

The pilot was in a hurry, and Chief Hewlett would accommodate him by taking unnecessary risks. Now I must say the Chief had been around and had seen this done before, but that did not seem like the right thing to do. His plan was for me to be inside the air intake and to watch for the leak as the pilot fired up the screaming jet engine.

What am I doing here?

I whispered, Dear Lord, help me.

The pilot looked intently at the Chief.

"Chief, are you sure about this?" asked the pilot.

"Sure, Yes Sir," replied Chief Hewlett.

"I have seen this done several times on the old F-9," he confirmed.

Chief Hewlett explained to the pilot that I would not be harmed, the turbine blades on this model of aircraft were encased with hardware cloth, (rat wire) and the worst thing that could happen was that I would be sucked up against the wire.

"Dear Lord, help me," I whispered.

Chief Hewlett had me empty my pockets of anything that could fly into the engine. He had a rope brought out, and had me tie it around my ankle, and gave me a pair of Mickey Mouse Ears (hearing protection head set), and asked the pilot to get in the plane and fire it up once I was inside the intake. He explained that the clam shell doors would open once the engine was running and give me light to see the leak.

The pilot looked at me standing by the intake with the rope tied to my leg and another sailor (Airman George Trump) holding the other end. He looked back at Chief Hewlett. I think the pilot prayed.

"Chief, are you sure about this?" he asked again.

"It will be just fine, Petty Officer Whitt will see the leak and we can get it fixed quickly," he said.

The stage was set, and the only one sure about things was the Chief. I was not too sure about it, who ever heard of a man being in the intake of a jet plane while the engine was being fired up.

"Lord, be with me," I whispered.

The pilot climbed into the cockpit and readied himself to fire the engine. Chief Hewlett nodded for me to crawl inside the intake. The sailor holding the rope stood to the side of the intake and fed the rope as I crawled to the very back of the metal tunnel, next to the engine. I must say I was having scary thoughts, being back inside the bowels of a war plane in the darkness and feeling the closeness of the tight space.

The Chief signaled the pilot to fire the engine. He fired it up and ran it up to a high RPM, before backing off to a steady run as they usually did.

The noise was horrific and the wind coming by me rolled up my bell bottom dungarees plumb past my knees. It took all I had not to panic. I trusted God!

The clam shell doors on top of the fuselage cracked open because of the lack of air to the great engine. I composed myself for an instant and looked around for a leak. There it was and I took a mental picture. I was done, get me out of this thing I signaled by trashing both legs against the inside of the tight intake.

The Chief signaled the pilot to shut it down and Airman Trump holding the rope began to pull me out. As I bent my body to allow my feet to touch the deck the Chief was laughing at the sight. My britches were rolled up past my knees, and my shirt was up around my neck. The chief saw my face and quit laughing.

"Did you find the leak?" Chief Hewlett asked.

"Yes I know where it is," I answered.

I patiently put myself back together, and untied the rope on my leg. Chief Hewlett and I got up on the wing and pushed down on the clam shell door. I pointed to the leak and jumped down off the F-9. The Chief showed the other sailor and he reached in and with his wrench tightened up the loose fitting. He next checked the reservoir and added fluid.

By now the pilot was on the deck and came over and personally thanked me for doing what I did. I acted brave, but it scared the stuffing's out of me. I decided that day that I would never do such a stunt again, no matter who ordered it. Thank God, I never panicked!

The pilot got back into his bird, and the crew sent him toward the runway. He gave me a wave, and I gave him a salute as he parted. So you see I was inside a jet plane, and didn't know if I would get out again. The more modern jets around the base would have chewed me up, and spit me out as burnt hamburger. I suggest you never try this at home. If you have to, be sure to take God with you!

Dahnmon Home From Boot Camp, Sep. 1964

What am I doing here?

Selfish Prayer

How often did I pray in my younger years? I prayed mostly when I needed a great big God to save my hind-end. Let's look at how Jesus taught us to pray!

"The Lord's Prayer"

Our Father, which art in heaven,
Hallowed be thy Name.
Thy Kingdom come.
Thy will be done on earth,
As it is in heaven.
Give us this day our daily bread.
And forgive us our trespasses,
As we forgive them that trespass against us.
And lead us not into temptation,
But deliver us from evil.
For thine is the kingdom,

The power, and the glory,

For ever and ever.

Amen.

Our Father: The Lord our God that created the Universe loves His children and will allow us to call Him, Father. Not only will He allow it, He wants to have us in that relationship where we want Him to be our Father. We are to start all of our prayers by Honoring and praising God our Heavenly Father.

Which Art In Heaven: Our God is in Heaven and sets on the throne as God of God, King of Kings. Is He here on earth also? Sure He is in the form of the Holy Spirit.

Hallowed be Thy Name: There is none higher and none that deserves more honor than God the Father, Jesus Christ the Son, or the Holy Spirit! That is why it is hard to understand why He is so concerned with mere people. We cannot Honor and praise Jesus Christ enough.

Thy Kingdom Come: Did you know you were praying for God's Kingdom to come? When we pray this prayer, we are asking Our Father to send the Son, Jesus Christ to claim His children. Even the animals and all of nature is calling out, "Please Come Father God."

Thy Will be done On Earth, as it is in Heaven:

I think we know that God rules all of Heaven. Now we want Him to take complete control in Earth and put Satan in bondage. If we pray for this, there will be peace and love in earth just like in Heaven. There will be no sin. Sin is the father of lies, cheating, stealing and murder. That will have to go, when our Father rules in Earth as in Heaven. I vote He does it!

Give us this day our daily bread:

Now we must be honest, where does our daily food come from? Did some farmer grow it? Sure the farmer grew it, He prepared the ground, he planted the seed, and God made it grow. Everything you have is given to you by your Heavenly Father, so ask Him for it and give Him thanks for all of His bounty.

And forgive us our trespasses, As we forgive them that trespass against us:

Now we are asking God to forgive our sins. Are we willing to forgive the sins of others? I am sorry to tell you this, but God will not forgive you of your sins, until you forgive your brothers sins. Jesus is always just and ready to forgive your sins and even forget your sins, but you must humble yourself and forgive all that have sinned against you. This is hard to do because we have been hurt by our friends or family by their sins.

And lead us not into temptation, but deliver us from evil:

Now this is one that I have really noticed. Pray that temptation be removed and pray that God will deliver you out of the hands of the evil one. First, don't go to someplace where you know you will be tempted to sin. And when Satan tricks you into sinning, ask God to get you out of harm's way.

Don't go to a place where women take off their clothes and expect not to be tempted. If you lust after one of these it is counted as adultery. Wow, did you know that? If you watch a movie and you think it is clean, fine, but if temptation jumps up to cause you to sin, turn it off! Can you do it? If your eye causes you to sin, what does the Bible say to do? Pluck it out! Do not deliberately sin! Let your conscience and the word of God be your guide.

For thine is the kingdom, the power, and the glory, For ever and ever:
We are recognizing the fact that God is in charge, He is almighty powerful and can speak things into existence. Pray that this will go on forever, because you want to live with Him forever. I know this is hard to understand, but God has prepared a place for His children. He has the power to see it through. And His kingdom will last forever. I am so glad that God loves His children and wants us to live with Him forever.

Amen!
So be it! It is true and this is how we should pray.
Prayer is the strongest Force on Earth, We connect directly to God.

Is God Watching Over You?

Start thinking back over your life, how many times have you come close to death and felt the presence of God save your butt?

I have mentioned a few close calls and I have a few more that is hard to explain, except through Divine Intervention.

Following are some more examples of how our Heavenly Father protects us.

My God hath sent his angel, and hath shut the lions mouths, that they have not hurt me: Daniel 6:22

What has God done for you? Has He ever saved your butt?

What am I doing here?

A Wave Of Destruction

While working in the Sheet Metal Trade, I
ran the Heating, Ventilating, Air-
conditioning work on the Ripley, Ohio High
School. This took place in 1991. This was a
long drive from home so I and a couple of
friends shared a camper and stayed right on
the job site. We worked four ten hour days
and headed home on Thursday evening each
week.

There was some good fishing on Eagle Creek
which emptied into the Ohio River less than
one half mile from the new school. This
would be our pastime each evening after
work. I brought my fourteen foot canoe, and
kept it ready on the ladder rack of the little
truck the company supplied me.

We started fishing just as soon as the
weather warmed up enough, and fished
almost every Monday, Tuesday, and
Wednesday evening all summer long. Eagle
Creek would rise and fall with the opening
and closing of the Dam Locks down river on

the Ohio, and stayed full a good mile upstream. We fished Eagle Creek most of the summer, but kept hearing about a good Creek downstream called Straight Creek.

Fishermen are like cattle in one way; they think the grass is greener on the other side of the fence; fishing is always better someplace else. We decided sometime in the near future we would travel to the other side of Ripley, and investigate the fishing possibilities on Straight Creek.

It was a hot muggy Wednesday afternoon about 5 PM when a thunder storm rolled in. The storm put a damper on our daily fishing. We went on to the camper, ate supper and cleaned up. The storm was just passing through and did not last very long. The Sun popped out with a blue sky and this put us to thinking. It would be muddy around Eagle Creek and we had already decided not to go fishing, but we could drive out and look at Straight Creek.

One of my friends, Jimmy wanted to wait by

the phone; his wife was expecting a new baby any day. Jay the other friend suggested that we go and take a look at Straight Creek.

Since I was curious about this new fishing possibility; I thought it was a good idea.

"Okay," I said, "we will just be looking, no need to take our fishing poles."

"Yes, let's take our poles and one lure, we might want to throw in a time or two," Jay answered.

We put our poles in the bed of the truck and drove down river a couple of miles to Straight Creek. Of course it was backed up because of the Ohio River Dam also. There was a nice marina set up with lots of boats. It looked like a lake. We followed the road around the deep water and started up the big hills that lay to the north of the Ohio River. We followed Straight Creek and it reminded me of some of the terrain in southwest Virginia and some of the trout streams I had fished. I guessed that we traveled about ten miles to a bridge that crossed the creek. We must have gained 500 feet in elevation since we left the road in Ripley.

We crossed the bridge and turned on to a dirt and gravel road that followed the creek downstream. I could not believe the beautiful mountain stream right here this close to the Ohio River. The creek was clear as a crystal and very rocky.

Jay and I found a wide spot on the road and parked the truck. We walked over to look at the beautiful creek. It was shallow for the most part, with long areas of water three to four feet deep. There was not much sign that it had even stormed.

Between each long hole the water flowed fast like a mountain stream in Virginia. There were many large, mostly flat limestone rocks in the creek and a limestone bottom. Jay and I got our fishing poles and found our way through the tall weeds and out on some of the rocks. The rocks were very slick.

"They should have named this Slippery Rock Creek," Jay said as he slipped along to another rock.

"You got that right!" I answered in agreement.

We started casting our baits out into the pools, and found that the creek was full of little Bass and Red Eyes. Most any place I tossed my artificial crawdad a fish hit it. We caught something just about every time we cast out. I could not believe, in less than an hour ago the sky was black and we had heavy rains back at the camper.

I saw a shadow or two in the deeper water that might be a bigger fish, so I waded out into the pool with the four to five feet bank on my left. I carefully and quietly went up stream into the quiet pool. As I concentrated on my fishing I heard an unusual noise. It was a real loud noise, like the roar of a big truck, yet I couldn't recognize it. I looked around to my right and several feet back at Jay that was in the middle of the creek on one of his slick rocks. The noisy became increasingly louder.

"What is that noise?" I hollered at Jay.

"Could be a truck," he said concentrating on his fishing.

The noise now became a roar. I looked back to Jay again. His eyes were opened wide as he looked franticly up stream.

"Get out of here, NOW!" he screamed and I turned back around to see what was going on up stream.

I could hardly comprehend what my eyes were telling me.

There was a wall of muddy water coming down the Creek that had to be 40 feet wide and ten feet tall. It was way up on each bank flattening the weeds, breaking down small trees and flipping large rocks like they were

What am I doing here?

pieces of paper. The sound now sounded like a jet plane taking off, and here I stood in 3 feet of water. The bank on my left was at least five feet high and covered with big creek weeds. It was at least 30 feet back down the creek over the slippery bottom to where I came in.

I Heard a Voice, **"Get up this bank now!"**

I had the fishing pole in my hand and somehow the crawdad plug hooked on to my shirt. I started to try to climb the steep bank, and got about a foot out of the water and slipped back into the water. I would have thrown away the fishing rod, but the fishing plug was hanging in my shirt and pricking at my chest.

I heard the voice again just as plain as could be, **"Get up this bank now!"**

It had to be God, my inner soul, or God's Angel saying it, but I think it was my Heavenly Father giving me fair warning. I put myself in four wheel drive grabbed anything that was available and dug myself up the steep bank. Just as I cleared the bank I lunged forward in great strides to higher ground. Just as I reached safety I turned around to see the great wave go by.

Jay had beat me out of harm's way by a few seconds and stood there hollering at me to hurry. He was in a much better place to evacuate the creek and avoid the danger.

I have heard of flash floods; some even take an hour to rise, but this was a Tsunami right here in Ohio. I have no doubt that God sent his Angel to save me that day.

Jay and I sat on the tailgate of the little truck to settle ourselves down. We could still find it hard to believe, what we had just witnessed. We were shook up the rest of the day. I prayed over and over thanking God for saving me that day.

When we got back to the camper, we could not come up with the words to fully describe what had happened, to our friend Jimmy.

We were back at work the following Monday and decided to go back and look at Straight Creek. The tall creek weeds were flattened out, great flat rocks had been flipped, and brush was hanging in limbs as high as 10 feet above the ground. We noticed dead crawfish everywhere and the beautiful pools that once held so many fish were now void of any fish.

As we looked around, I couldn't help but look up the creek, afraid there might be another great wave of water to shun.

To this day I have never heard what caused the Tsunami on Straight Creek. Was there a dam that gave way, or was there a cloudburst up stream that caused such a flash flood?

God was not through with me, so he sent His Angel to rescue me on that faithful day and other days also.

For he shall give his angels charge over thee, to keep thee in all thy ways. Psalm 91:11

I have had several close to death chances where I believe God stepped in. I was working on a decked roof at a Boyd, County school several years ago. The roof was not installed at this time only the decking. I did not know it at the time, but the decking was not complete either.

My boss George and I were setting huge HVAC equipment with a very large crane. The curbs were in place so all we had to do was maneuver the units over the curbs and ease them down.

When working and rigging large loads and handling them with a crane you must practice top notch safety procedures.

One of the huge HVAC units was over the roof but too high for me to get a hand on. It is standard practice to back out from under any large loads in case there was a mishap.

The crane could break down or the rigging could come lose and if you are under it, you get the picture.

I was backing out and waiting for it to get closer to the roof so I could guide it to the curb.

"Charlie, Charlie, freeze," screamed my friend George.

I listened, stopped, and turned to look behind me. There it was a big hole in the roof that had not been decked. One more step backward and I would have plunged 30 feet to the concrete deck.

I moved away from the opening and went over to a pile of hard roofing insulation, on my wobbling legs and set down.

I knew instantly how close I came to certain death. I thanked God as I recovered.

George said he didn't know why he looked my way because he had been concentrating on the big HVAC unit. I know, my guardian Angel intervened, because God was not through with me.

Another time I was working on the roof of Harlan, Kentucky High School. The HVAC units had been set and we were assembling other parts that didn't come pre-assembled. The roof was rubber and it had been applied. The ballast for the roof was one to two inch stones and was not applied. The stone was in piles all over the roof and was waiting for the roofers to spread it out all evenly over the roof.

A coworker and I were carrying a bulky economizer made of sheet metal. It was heavy and hard to carry. I was only two feet from the edge of the roof when I stepped up on one of the piles of stone. The weight of the piece and the uneven footing put all the weight on the heel of my right foot. A little bone snapped and at that moment when I should have fallen right and off the roof, I felt something push me to the left and to safety. Sure I had a broken foot, but I did

What am I doing here?

not fall off of the high roof. God was with me all that day because I felt his loving spirit and knew my guardian angel had been at work again.

I bet if you would think back, you have had several near-misses also. I truly have too many to mention and have not been as close to God as I should have.

Let's Look At Sin and Grace

This is a faithful saying, and worthy of all acceptation, that Christ Jesus came into the world to save sinners; of whom I am chief. I Tim. 1:15.

This verse is quoted to prove that no matter how much grace one has received from the Lord yet he can never get beyond the place where he is reckoned a sinner. "If Paul said he was the chief of sinners, then how dare we, with so much less grace and salvation, lay claim to anything higher?

Let us examine Paul a little. If he meant here that he, at this time, was the chief of sinners, let us see how this statement harmonizes with the rest of his teaching. Paul was an apostle. He wrote upon one occasion that he supposed he *"was not a whit (least inferior) behind the very top chief of the apostles. 2 Cor. 11:5.*

It is true that in his humility he said he was "less than the least of all saints," when he considered what a sinner he had been, and how the Lord had saved him and exalted him to preach "the unreachable riches of Christ; but even in this humble statement he confessed that he is a saint, which means a holy person, and, to say the least, it is above being the chief of sinners.

He said that he was "allowed of God to be put in trust with the Gospel." We cannot understand how God could choose a man to be an apostle and commit unto him the Gospel to preach, knowing that he was the chief of sinners.

He wrote on another occasion that the mystery was *"revealed unto the holy apostles." Eph. 3:5.*

This, of course, included himself, as he was an apostle. Here is a profession of holiness from Paul. It sounds somewhat different from being the chief of sinners.

3. Paul told the Thessalonian church, *"Ye are witnesses and God also, how holily and*

justly and not blamed we behaved ourselves among you that believe."
Ist. Thessalonians 2:10.

Suppose that he had added in the next verse, that he was the chief of sinners, how would they have reconciled the statement?

In another place Paul made a profession of Christian perfection: *"Let us therefore, as many as be perfect, be thus minded."*
Phil. 3:15.

Paul thus classes himself with those who had obtained this perfection. The chief of sinners would hardly harmonize in this piece.

He wrote to the Romans and said: *"I am sure, that when I come unto you, I shall come in the fullness of the blessing of the Gospel of Christ."* Rom. 15:29.

How can one be in the fullness of the blessing of Christ, and at the same time be the chief of sinners?

In another place he writes that he is crucified with Christ, and that Christ is living in him. Gal. 2:20. <u>One of the strongest expressions of full salvation. Is the chief of sinners crucified with Christ, and possessed with the Christ life?</u>

He won hundreds to Christ and led many into the baptism with the Holy Ghost. How could one continually succeed in raising men to a higher level than himself? How could one, the chief of sinners, succeed in getting other sinners to God and then in getting them filled with the Holy Ghost?

God trusted Paul to write a portion of the inspired Word; committed unto him a dispensation of the Gospel through him wrought miracles of different kinds. Can we imagine a Holy God committing such sacred works to the chief of sinners?

The very next year after Paul wrote this text about the chief of sinners he wrote: *"For I am now ready to be offered and the time of my departure is at hand. I have fought a good fight, I have finished my course, I have kept the faith; henceforth there is laid up for me a crown of righteousness, which the Lord, the righteous judge, shall give me at that day; end not to me only, but unto them also that love His appearing."* 2 Tim. 4:6-8.

How could the chief of sinners say, as he was facing death, that he had fought a good fight, and kept the faith, and was expecting a crown of righteousness? Is a crown of righteousness laid up for sinners?

Paul wrote, *"Awake to righteousness, and sin not."* I Cor. 15:34.

And again he asks the question, *"What shall we say then? Shall we continue in sin that grace may abound? God forbid. How shall we, that are dead to sin, live any longer therein?"* Rom. 6:1-2.

Strange that Paul should exhort others to quit sinning and keep right on himself. Where would be the consistency?

We read in the Word that *"Sin is the transgression of the law."* Also, *"to him that knoweth to do good, and doeth it not, to him it is sin."*

Therefore now, if Paul was the chief of sinners, then he was a transgressor of the law. This would prove hypocrisy in him; teaching others what he himself did not live up to. If he knew to do good and did it not, which he did if he were the chief of sinners, then how could he be holy, and just, and not blamed, as he declared he was? This would certainly brand him as false, if he were then the chief of sinners.

Long years before Paul wrote the text in question he repented of his sins. Christ met him on the road to Damascus, struck him down under a mighty load of conviction.

"This is a faithful saying, and worthy of all acceptation, that Christ Jesus came into the world to save sinners; of whom I am chief." I Tim. 1:15.

Now how about me and you, are we also great sinners?

Have you broken any one of the Ten Commandments? If you felt like it was wrong, it probably was a sin. I know and confess that I have broken most of them if not all and still claim to be a son of God.

The apostle Paul understood our predicament. He told the Romans, *"I have the desire to do what is good, but I cannot carry it out. For what I do is not the good I want to do; no, the evil I do not want to do-this I keep on doing"* (Romans 7:18-19).

Does this sound like your life?

I'm not suggesting that Paul struggled with compulsive sexual behavior, but he did struggle with sin just like the rest of us. And like the rest of us, he would make up his mind not to commit a certain sin ever again. Did he succeed? No way! Now, if the apostle Paul couldn't overpower his sin, why should you and I think we can?

From the moment we get up in the morning until we climb between the sheets at night, we're bombarded with erotic images and messages.

Suppose you made up your mind you were going to make it through one day without lusting after a woman. On your way to work your eyes are drawn to the bikini-clad model greeting you from a billboard. A few moments later as you stop at an intersection, you aren't able to keep from noticing the attractively dressed young woman crossing the street.

At work a friend brags about the gorgeous babe he bedded the night before. As you order lunch, the waitress with the short skirt winks at you and smiles. When you get back to the office, a coworker eagerly shows you his favorite erotic image on the Internet.

On your way home you stop at the grocery store and catch yourself gazing at the seminude models that adorn the magazines by the checkout counter.

When you finally get home, you plop down in an easy chair and flip on the TV. As you channel surf, you're exposed to more of the female anatomy than I found in the pages of Playboy when I was a kid.

With the high level of erotic stimulation you face on a daily basis, do you believe you can bridle your lust alone? I remember a friend once telling me (and he said this with a straight face), "I'll never have a problem with sexual lust."

I looked at him and said, "You're absolutely amazing. If that's true, you're stronger than Samson, godlier that David, and wiser than Solomon."

I'll never forget his response. He sat down and stared at me for a half minute without uttering a word. And then he said, "I never thought of it like that."

I'll guarantee you, if Samson, David, and Solomon were here, they'd all say, "You can't defeat your lust alone!"

Only Christ can help you, not to sin, and yet you will fall again. Do we have a sinning religion? No, we are weak and Jesus Christ has the power to guide us away from the devil. When we fall, the Grace of Jesus will be there to forgive us. Do not sin!

Strive for perfection, do not expect to fail, but know that Jesus is just and always ready to take a repenting sinner back.

I love that part of the Lord's Prayer that asks God to deliver us from evil and to lead us not into temptation. Now this works, but we must mean it and rely on God. Yet we will fall again as the devil is a crafty old fallen angel.

I am Mortal

I am not going to tell you about my every sin, but will touch on some so that you can relate to your own sins.

I have always liked girls as far back as I remember. Some of the first things I learned to write were "I Love You," and "Hugs and Kisses."

I didn't know why I did a lot of the things I did. I learned to lie, at an early age. I also learned to steal, nothing big, but to God sin is sin.

I guess I started noticing the girls in a different way at about the 5th grade. In the 6th grade, I moved up to admiring my beautiful teacher. I was not the only boy that loved her. I was sort off a pet. She called me her "Dahnmon."

I will have to admit that if she was like some of the teachers today, we may have been in some trouble. She was just a nice lady, the rest was in my head, I think.

We kids began some experiments in kissing. We loved to play the kissing games like "Spin The Bottle," and "Post Office."

I went to visit my cousin one summer with my grandmother and had a ball. My little girl cousin loved to kiss as much as me. We kissed all week. It was a good thing we were too young to think of other things.

Jesus said if you lust after a woman in your heart it is the same as committing adultery. If you covet (want) what your neighbor has, it is just like stealing.

I disobeyed my Mom and Dad by doing thing I shouldn't. I tried smoking, and even tried chewing tobacco at an early age. Some of my so called friends tempted me to chew a big cud of tobacco and swallow the juice. I was sick as could be, but could not tell my parents.

Now don't you think these boys did some sinning to get me sick like that?

Now think about the boy Jesus, was he tempted like I was? According to the word of God, Jesus was tempted and never sinned. We have to believe that Jesus never sinned; He is the perfect sacrifice to redeem our sin.

As I grew into a man my thoughts became sinful in a bigger way. I learned about jealousy, about lust, about hiding my sin and about committing a number of other sins. I did not rob banks or kill folks, but none the less I sinned. I learned to love the darkness of night so I could hide my sins I committed with girls and I also did some drinking of the spirits. I liked to drive at high speeds and hated the police for trying to catch me at it. I was past the age of accountability and from time to time my conscience would reel me in. I still went to church most of the time, but I wasn't too fond of it. I knew I did wrong many times and would occasionally pray for forgiveness. This happened mostly when things were not going my way.

 Wait just a minute, am I the only person to go through this? You know this happened to some great men in the Bible. Now I know I have a chance to end up right with God.

Dahnmon at an early age.

David and Bathsheba

2 Samuel 11:1:

1. Then it happened in the spring, at the time when kings go out to battle, that David sent Joab and his servants with him and all Israel, and they destroyed the sons of Ammon and besieged Rabbah. But David stayed at Jerusalem.

At the very root of David's problems, we find a king who wasn't where he belonged. If David had been out in the battlefield, where the king was supposed to be, instead of hanging around the palace looking at naked women; this whole incident would have never happened.

Some have suggested that David may have been battling depression, or having a "mid-life crisis." In either event, he wasn't where he belonged; which, at least in my life, is often the first step of a downhill slide.

2. Now when evening came David arose from his bed and walked around on the roof

What am I doing here?

of the king's house, and from the roof he saw a woman bathing; and the woman was very beautiful in appearance.

3. So David sent and inquired about the woman. And one said, "Is this not Bathsheba, the daughter of Eliam, the wife of Uriah the Hittite?"

4 David sent messengers and took her, and when she came to him, he lay with her; and when she had purified herself from her uncleanness, she returned to her house.

I should point out here that, when viewed through the eyes of modern western civilization, it's all too easy to conclude that Bathsheba shares in David's guilt as a willing participant, or if nothing else, an immodest woman who had no business bathing where the King could see her. To be honest, I've even taught that perspective in the past, but I've also been gently but firmly corrected for my error. In that society's governmental system, the King was the absolute authority. If Bathsheba was summoned to the King's palace, then she came to the palace or risked execution for defying the King. Bathsheba's bathing was not in a public place, but probably behind the walls of an enclosed courtyard. She had no expectation that she would be seen, since the King was, after all, supposed to be out in the battlefield with her husband. Clearly, this is a case of one man abusing his power to satisfy his own lustful desires.

David didn't set out to commit an insidious sin. People seldom do. At first inquiry, he didn't know this woman's identity or her marital status. Had she been unmarried, he would have been quite proper in pursuing her as a wife and his inquiry would not have been improper. By the time he learned that she was married, David had already let lust get its nasty little hooks into his heart, and his lustful desire outweighed his good sense and integrity. Unbridled lust can do that to a person; yes, even you, if you allow it to smolder long enough.

By this point, it's apparent that David's intentions have shifted from an interest in taking Bathsheba as a wife, to just plain taking Bathsheba. David had no plans on a long term affair; just a one-night sexual romp with a good-looking woman.

As usual, sin had its consequences:

5 The woman conceived; and she sent and told David, and said, "I am pregnant."

Oops. David hadn't planned on that possibility. We never do when we are under strong temptation.

Have you ever committed adultery? I bet you have, maybe not physically. <u>If you thought it; you done it!</u> That is just the way it is.

How will David get out of this one?

David had sinned, and as usual, sin had its consequences:

5 The woman conceived; and she sent and told David, and said, "I am pregnant."

David, demonstrating that he was just like the rest of us, went with his first instinct; he tried to cover up his sin and shift the responsibility to someone else.

6 Then David sent to Joab, saying, "Send me Uriah the Hittite." So Joab sent Uriah to David.

7 When Uriah came to him, David asked concerning the welfare of Joab and the people and the state of the war.

8 Then David said to Uriah, "Go down to your house, and wash your feet." And Uriah went out of the king's house and a present from the king was sent out after him.

9 But Uriah slept at the door of the king's house with all the servants of his lord, and did not go down to his house.

What am I doing here?

10 Now when they told David, saying, "Uriah did not go down to his house," David said to Uriah, "Have you not come from a journey? Why did you not go down to your house?"

11 Uriah said to David, "The ark and Israel and Judah are staying in temporary shelters, and my lord Joab and the servants of my lord are camping in the open field. Shall I then go to my house to eat and to drink and to lie with my wife? By your life and the life of your soul, I will not do this thing."

12 Then David said to Uriah, "Stay here today also, and tomorrow I will let you go." So Uriah remained in Jerusalem that day and the next.

13 Now David called him, and he ate and drank before him, and he made him drunk; and in the evening he went out to lie on his bed with his lord's servants, but he did not go down to his house.

Uriah, Bathsheba's husband, was a faithful warrior who was out on the battlefield; the same battlefield where David should have been. David called Uriah in from the battle, probably under the disguise of a special project or task (not really a "lie" in legalese thinking; it was a special project for the king, in a warped sort of way).

After a few pleasantries and war stories, he told Uriah to go down to his house, assuming of course that Uriah would have marital relations with Bathsheba while he was home, which would allow him to think that the baby was his, effectively covering up the incident.

The one thing that they didn't consider in the plan was Uriah's sense of honor and loyalty. He would not go and enjoy the pleasures of home when his fellow-soldiers were camping in the battlefield. David even tried getting him drunk, but Uriah's sense of duty and honor was strong enough to overcome all of David's tactics.

Finally, David gets desperate, and like most desperate men, did something stupid:

14 Now in the morning David wrote a letter to Joab and sent it by the hand of Uriah.

15 He had written in the letter, saying, "Place Uriah in the front line of the fiercest battle and withdraw from him, so that he may be struck down and die."

David sent word back to Joab, the leader of the king's army, to put Uriah in a place where he would be killed. Although he did not know why the king had ordered Uriah's death, Joab obeyed his king's command, probably under the assumption that the king had good reason, and that perhaps Uriah had somehow been disloyal to the kingdom.

16 So it was as Joab kept watch on the city, that he put Uriah at the place where he knew there were valiant men.

17 The men of the city went out and fought against Joab, and some of the people among David's servants fell; and Uriah the Hittite also died.

It appears that the only way that Joab could arrange for the death of a seasoned warrior such as Uriah was to use some unwise battle tactics, which caused several good men to die with him. Cover-ups are often like that; a lot of innocent people get hurt while we are trying to hide the truth. Joab was so sure that David would react poorly to the battle strategy that led to Uriah's death that, when the messenger went to update David on the war, Joab gave him specific instructions that would tell David that the deed had been done.

18 Then Joab sent and reported to David all the events of the war.

19 He charged the messenger, saying, "When you have finished telling all the events of the war to the king,

What am I doing here?

20 and if it happens that the king's wrath rises and he says to you, 'Why did you go so near to the city to fight? Did you not know that they would shoot from the wall?

21 Who struck down Abimelech the son of Jerubbesheth? Did not a woman throw an upper millstone on him from the wall so that he died at Thebez? Why did you go so near the wall? Then you shall say, "Your servant Uriah the Hittite is dead also."

22 So the messenger departed and came and reported to David all that Joab had sent him to tell.

23 The messenger said to David, "The men prevailed against us and came out against us in the field, but we pressed them as far as the entrance of the gate."

24 "Moreover, the archers shot at your servants from the wall; so some of the king's servants are dead, and your servant Uriah the Hittite is also dead."

25 Then David said to the messenger, "Thus you shall say to Joab, "Do not let this thing displease you, for the sword devours one as well as another; make your battle against the city stronger and overthrow it" and so encourage him."

It's interesting that Joab knew David well enough to anticipate his reaction to the strategic error, but there is no evidence that David even flinched at the news. David's focus was on one thing, and only one thing, hiding his sin, at any cost. Matters of state and ethical issues had been pushed down on David's priority list.

Now, with Uriah out of the way, David could make the cover-up complete:

26 Now when the wife of Uriah heard that Uriah her husband was dead, she mourned for her husband.

27 When the time of mourning was over, David sent and brought her to his house and she became his wife; then she bore him a son. But the thing that David had done was evil in the sight of the LORD.

Bathsheba mourned for her husband, as was proper. Then, as a gesture of supposed nobility, the king took the poor widow in and made her one of his wives. My, what a noble gesture, in today's world, the king's press agent would have made it a photo-op, and gotten it on the front page of every newspaper in the land.

David thought the whole incident was covered. The only living person who knew the entire truth and could testify against him was Bathsheba, and her silence was probably motivated by fear for her own life. There also were some men who served the king, who had partial knowledge, but they remained loyal to the king even when he was wrong and were probably compensated for their silence. All of his bases were covered or so he thought. He only overlooked one small detail; you can't hide your heart from God.

David had sinned, and thought that he had managed to build an effective cover-up plan.

12:1 Then the LORD sent Nathan to David. And he came to him and said, "There were two men in one city, the one rich and the other poor.

2 The rich man had a great many flocks and herds.

3 But the poor man had nothing except one little ewe lamb which he bought and nourished; and it grew up together with him and his children. It would eat of his bread and drink of his cup and lie in his bosom, and was like a daughter to him.

4 "Now a traveler came to the rich man, And he was unwilling to take from his own flock or his own herd, To prepare for the wayfarer who had come to him; rather he took the poor man's ewe lamb and prepared it for the man who had come to him."

What am I doing here?

5 Then David's anger burned greatly against the man, and he said to Nathan, "As the LORD lives, surely the man who has done this deserves to die."

6 "He must make restitution for the lamb fourfold, because he did this thing and had no compassion."

Nathan's parable was a close parallel to what David had done and had covered up so skillfully. This should remind us that, no matter how hard we try, we can't hide from God. We're much better off if we're just honest with Him up front, it's not like He doesn't already know.

Nathan set David up, and David took the bait. David still had a moral conscience even though he had ignored it in his own situation and that moral conscience screamed for justice. David, as king, had authority to pronounce judgment on such criminals and that's exactly what he did; not realizing that he was pronouncing his own judgment the death penalty.

It was then, in verse 7, that Nathan brought it to light!

7 Nathan then said to David, "You are the man! Thus says the LORD God of Israel, It is I who anointed you king over Israel and it is I who delivered you from the hand of Saul.

8 I also gave you your master's house and your master's wives into your care, and I gave you the house of Israel and Judah; and if that had been too little I would have added to you many more things like these!

9 Why have you despised the word of the LORD by doing evil in His sight? You have struck down Uriah the Hittite with the sword; have taken his wife to be your wife, and have killed him with the sword of the sons of Ammon.

10 Now therefore, the sword shall never depart from your house, because you have despised Me and have taken the wife of Uriah the Hittite to be your wife.

11 Thus says the LORD, Behold, I will raise up evil against you from your own household; I will even take your wives before your eyes and give them to your companion, and he will lie with your wives in broad daylight.

12 Indeed you did it secretly but I will do this thing before all Israel and under the sun.

David was reminded, as I often need to be, that God is bigger and smarter than we are. Nathan, who hadn't been a party to any of this incident, recited back to David EXACTLY what he had done, in painful detail, and pronounced God's judgment on the king. On top of that, David had already pronounced his own death sentence; he was backed into an uncomfortable corner.

It's important to understand the dynamic of this situation. Nathan literally risked his life bringing this accusation before the king. The king was the sole power of government; he could have told one of the guards to kill Nathan on the spot. He could have denied his sin, and argued with Nathan (and with God).

He could have defied them and continued in his denial. The choice was David's to make. Nathan understood the risk yet also understood that obedience to God, even to the point of death, is better than long life of rebellion and disobedience.

David's truth and obedience; "a man after God's own heart" rose up within him. David came face-to-face with himself, made the noblest statement of his life:

13 Then David said to Nathan, "I have sinned against the LORD." (2 Samuel 12:13a)

There was none of the blame-shifting "but" phrases that typified Saul, his predecessor to the throne. There were no excuses, no spin, no double-talk or waffling. David saw his situation clearly, and dealt with it boldly.

With his admission of guilt, it would have been fully justified if God had carried out the sentence pronounced upon him by his own judgment and struck him dead on the spot. David confessed his sin, and expected to die for it.

It is when we are truly honest with God that we find His mercy and grace:

And Nathan said to David, "The LORD also has taken away your sin; you shall not die." (2 Samuel 12:13b)

This was an important defining moment in David's life. He confessed his sin, and was prepared to accept his punishment of death. Instead, God showed His grace by forgiving David, and allowing him to live. For the rest of his days, when David opened his eyes in the morning, he knew that he was alive for one reason and one reason only; the sheer grace of God. That turning point changed the direction of David's life, and deepened his relationship with God to a level he had never known before. Understanding God's grace will have the same effect on you and me.

Psalm 51 is David's prayer of repentance. It illustrates that David's repentance was not just a "sorry, I'll try to do better" sort of thing, but a deep, heartfelt plea to God for forgiveness, healing and restoration.

We all have this chance while we still breathe. We must admit that we are sinners and need God's Grace.

Psalm 51
1 Be gracious to me, O God, according to Your loving-kindness; According to the greatness of Your compassion blot out my transgressions.

2 Wash me thoroughly from my iniquity And cleanse me from my sin.

3 For I know my transgressions, And my sin is ever before me.

David didn't try to shift the blame for his sin. This Psalm doesn't contain one single word of self-justification. David didn't try to blame Bathsheba for his downfall, or talk about the enormous stresses and responsibilities in the life of a great leader. He faced his sin head-on, and called it what it was: his sin.

4 Against You, You only, I have sinned And done what is evil in Your sight, So that You are justified when You speak And blameless when You judge.

David understood that, while he had indeed sinned against Uriah and Bathsheba, any sin is first and foremost a sin against God, and his first step of repentance is confession before God.

5 Behold, I was brought forth in iniquity, and in sin my mother conceived me.

6 Behold, You desire truth in the innermost being, And in the hidden part You will make me know wisdom.

David acknowledged the basic depravity of mankind, himself included. He finally came to the point of "truth in the inmost being," and was honest with himself about his sin.

7 Purify me with hyssop, and I shall be clean; Wash me, and I shall be whiter than snow.

Hyssop was used under Old Testament law for two rituals of purification. It was part of the purification of one healed of leprosy, and of those who had contact with a dead body. David saw his sin for what it really was: a deadly disease that could be cured only by God himself. Only the Grace of God can purify us and forgive our sins.

8 Make me to hear joy and gladness, Let the bones which You have broken rejoice.

9 Hide your face from my sins and blot out all my iniquities.

What am I doing here?

10 Create in me a clean heart, O God, and renew a steadfast spirit within me.

11 Do not cast me away from your presence and do not take Your Holy Spirit from me.

12 Restore to me the joy of your salvation and sustain me with a willing spirit.

David "prayed through" to the outcome of genuine repentance before God: that which was broken begins to heal, as God blots out our sin and creates a clean heart within us.

David's reference to being "cast away from your presence" in verse 11 refers back to his predecessor to the throne, King Saul, who failed to honestly repent of his sin of disobedience. As a result, God withdrew his Spirit from Saul, who lived out his days in misery and torment. David witnessed this chapter in Saul's life, and asked not only for forgiveness but for a renewed relationship, and deliverance from the fate of Saul.

13 Then I will teach transgressors your ways, And sinners will be converted to You.

14 Deliver me from blood-guiltiness, O God, the God of my salvation; then my tongue will joyfully sing of your righteousness.

15 O Lord, open my lips, that my mouth may declare your praise.

16 For you do not delight in sacrifice, otherwise I would give it; you are not pleased with burnt offering.

17 The sacrifices of God are a broken spirit; a broken and a contrite heart, O God, You will not despise.

18 By Your favor do good to Zion; Build the walls of Jerusalem.

19 Then you will delight in righteous sacrifices, in burnt offering and whole burnt offering; then young bulls will be offered on your altar.

What am I doing here?

<u>Genuine repentance brings forgiveness, restoration and healing,</u> and the end result of that cycle is action. David committed himself to serving God with his restored life, and leading other needy people to Him. It is not the "sacrifice" of labor that produces favor with God; it is favor with God, through honest repentance, that produces a willing servant.

Now, there are many who want the story to end with 2 Samuel 12:13, but don't stop reading; God's not finished yet! In fact, He's just getting started!

<u>So far, David has committed adultery, then ordered the murder of several innocent men, trying to cover up his sin. God has sent Nathan the Prophet to confront David, and David has sought God's forgiveness and expressed an attitude of genuine repentance.</u>

13 Then David said to Nathan, "I have sinned against the LORD." And Nathan said to David, "The LORD also has taken away your sin; you shall not die."

We love stories with perfect, happy endings, and we want sin forgiven without consequence. In reality, we can be forgiven for breaking the window, but we still have to sweep up the broken glass and repair the window. There are consequences to our actions, and like it or not, we must coexist with those consequences, just as David did.

2 Samuel 12:14 "However, because by this deed you have given occasion to the enemies of the LORD to blaspheme, the child also that is born to you shall surely die."

15 So Nathan went to his house. Then the LORD struck the child that Uriah's widow bore to David, so that he was very sick.

16 David therefore inquired of God for the child; and David fasted and went and lay all night on the ground.

What am I doing here?

17 The elders of his household stood beside him in order to raise him up from the ground but he was unwilling and would not eat food with them.

18 Then it happened on the seventh day that the child died. And the servants of David were afraid to tell him that the child was dead, for they said, "Behold, while the child was still alive, we spoke to him and he did not listen to our voice. How then can we tell him that the child is dead, since he might do himself harm!"

19 But when David saw that his servants were whispering together, David perceived that the child was dead; so David said to his servants, "Is the child dead?" And they said, "He is dead."

20 So David arose from the ground, washed, anointed himself, and changed his clothes; and he came into the house of the LORD and worshiped. Then he came to his own house, and when he requested, they set food before him and he ate.

21 Then his servants said to him, "What is this thing that you have done? While the child was alive, you fasted and wept; but when the child died, you arose and ate food."

22 He said, "While the child was still alive, I fasted and wept; for I said, 'Who knows, the LORD may be gracious to me, that the child may live.'

23 "But now he has died; why should I fast? Can I bring him back again? I will go to him, but he will not return to me." (2 Samuel 12:14-23).

The death of David's newborn son seems, at first look, to be a cruel and unfair punishment of an innocent child. The child's death does, however, underscore an important truth; our sin affects not only ourselves, but also those around us. The long-reaching effect of a moment of sinful self-indulgence can be disastrous. We seldom pause to consider that factor in a moment of

What am I doing here?

temptation. If we could see the results of our actions clearly, we'd say "NO" more often.

There were other consequences, too. The judgment proclaimed in verses 11 and 12 came to pass, when in 2 Samuel 16:20-22 David's rebellious son Absalom publicly went in to his father's wives and concubines to demonstrate his rebellion to the nation.

In verse 12, Nathan told David that what he tried to keep as a secret affair would be made public, and he would face public disgrace and humiliation. Bathsheba, though a part of the king's household, had to live with humiliation and disgrace in the midst of the king's other wives and concubines. In the terms of their society, the loss of a son was a sign of God's judgment upon them that was a matter of deep, scarring disgrace.

The best news of all is that the story does not end with the consequences of sin. Where there is sin, there are consequences, but where there is grace, there is; restoration and healing.

24 Then David comforted his wife Bathsheba, and went in to her and lay with her; and she gave birth to a son, and he named him Solomon. Now the LORD loved him

25 and sent word through Nathan the prophet, and he named him Jedidiah for the LORD'S sake.

I would have expected the embarrassed and disgraced Bathsheba to tell David that he could just stay on his side of the palace, and that she never wanted to lay eyes on him again. Perhaps she even did. Scripture does not record Bathsheba's journey of healing as it does David's, but there is sound evidence that she did repent and also forgive.

Who would think that a relationship with such a sin-drenched foundation could even survive, much less prosper?

What am I doing here?

God demonstrated His grace in the sanctification of a relationship that had once brought the condemnation of death. This is not a "healed but always deficient" relationship, but a "healed and holy household," a union that brought forth Solomon, a child regarded by both sacred and secular authority as one of the wisest men ever born. He succeeded his father as King, and his name appears in the direct bloodline of Christ in the New Testament genealogies.

The restored, healed, sanctified marriage of David and Bathsheba bears both God's hand and His blessing. It is purely poetic that the same prophet chosen to bring God's condemnation of sin was also chosen to deliver God's blessing on the fruits of this healed, holy relationship. The LORD sent word through Nathan that He had a special name for this special child: Jedidiah which means "beloved of God." It is important to note that the healing and reconstruction of this relationship did not happen immediately. Based on historical accounts and comparative scriptural studies, it is apparent that several years passed between the death of the first son and the birth of Solomon. It is also apparent that, although David had many wives, Bathsheba became his favorite. A marriage built on the healing grace of God always produces very special, intimate, bonded relationships.

God never brings us condemnation without offering us grace and healing. This is a recurring theme throughout the Bible; God wants to have an intimate relationship with each of us, and goes out of His way to invite us into that relationship. The whole point of Nathan's charge against David was not to punish him, but to restore him.

Are you ready for a fresh start? Your life can be healed, restored, and rebuilt, just like David's was. I can tell you from experience that it will not be an easy journey, but it will be the most worthwhile venture of your entire lifetime.

Like David, you will have to be honest with God, and with yourself.

You may say, "I have not murdered, I have not committed adultery."

I say you have sinned and need forgiveness, remember in the Book of Romans, it says "All have sinned and fall short of the glory of God."

I am so pleased to know that we have a loving God that offers us a hand up, when we fall down.

As we look at King David we see all aspects of Life's Journey. We see a boy chosen and anointed to serve as king of his nation. We see this boy being so brave because he knew God was with him. He killed a lion, a bear, and also a giant and delivered his nation.

We see David tempted and yielding to sin. To cover up this sin David tried a couple of devious things that eventually led to the death of several soldiers and also the husband of Bathsheba. His sin hurt many people, and especially God.

We see David caught up in sin by God and at once he confessed and repented. He knew he most likely would die for this sin. Our gracious God forgave David many times as he (David) was wise to humble himself and ask God to forgive him.

Here God forgave a murderer, and an adulterer, and a liar. God even called David, "A man after God's own heart."

Why is this? David knew to repent and humbly ask God for mercy. Do we have that same chance? You betcha!

My place of worship, Mead Memorial United Methodist Church, Russell Kentucky

My life and probably yours is like a roller coaster. We go up and down between light and darkness. I have found out it is much better in the light. I have seen both sides.

AMAZING GRACE

Genesis 19:19, *"Behold now, thy servant hath found grace in thy sight, and thou hast magnified thy mercy, which thou hast shewed unto me in saving my life;"*

John 1:14, *"And the Word was made flesh, and dwelt among us, (and we beheld his glory, the glory as of the only begotten of the Father,) full of grace and truth."*

Ephes. 2:7-8, *"That in the ages to come he might shew the exceeding riches of his grace in his kindness toward us through Christ Jesus. For by grace are ye saved through faith; and that not of yourselves: it is the gift of God:"*

Everybody, Christian and non-Christian alike have heard the song Amazing Grace. Few though know the story behind the song and the author-John Newton.

Death took his saintly mother in July, 1732 when John was but 13 days short of his 7th birthday. Newton wrote of his mother;

What am I doing here?

"Almost her whole employment was the care of my education. She stored my memory with many valuable pieces, chapters and portions of Scripture, hymns and poems."

After her death Newton went to sea with his father and began a decline into rebellion and degradation that lasted until he was 23 years old. His willful and wanton disregard for all that was right and holy led him into a life plagued with despair, dangers at sea, abuse, public floggings, and depression, near drowning's and miraculous escapes. It is reported that at times he was so wretched that even his crew regarded him as little more than an animal.

At the age of 23 Newton found himself on a small island off North Africa. He had contracted an illness that left him burning up with fever.

He wrote; *"Weak and almost delirious, I arose from my bed and crept to a secluded part of the island; there I found a renewed liberty to pray. I made no more resolves, but cast myself before the Lord to do with me as He should please. I was enabled to hope and believe in a crucified Savior."*

For the next sixteen years he married and studied for the ministry. At the age of 39 he became a pastor in Olney, England. In 1779 Newton published a hymnal **"The Olney Hymns"** in which he placed 281 of his own works, including his life's story, *"Amazing Grace."*

Anticipating HIS Soon Return,
By: Chaplain Alan Farley D.D.

I added this to show what and how God's Grace can make a difference in our lives. This John Newton has left us a great example to follow. We see where he sinned and where he came to himself. Have you come to yourself as yet? Have you saw the Light?

May God bless all that read this little book!

Other Books by:
Colonel Charles Dahnmon Whitt

"Legacy, The Days Of David Crockett Whitt"

"The Patriot, Hezekiah Whitt"

"Dahnmon's Little Stories"

"Confederate American"

"Haunts And Spirits Of The Past"

"The South Won, What If?"

"Legacy 2nd Edition"

For more information go to my site at
http://dahnmonwhittfamily.com/

Call at 606 836 7997 or write to:
Colonel Charles Dahnmon Whitt
Post Office Box 831
Flatwoods, Kentucky 41139-0831

E-Mail c-dahnmon@roadrunner.com

www.ingramcontent.com/pod-product-compliance
Lightning Source LLC
Chambersburg PA
CBHW081151090426
42736CB00017B/3272